Made in the USA
Las Vegas, NV
15 August 2024

93902747R00056